RE-STARTING YOUR DREAM FOR ADULTS

Dreams Are Timeless

Arlette Thomas-Fletcher

ISBN: 978-0-9715510-8-4

Publisher: Arlette Thomas-Fletcher

Shining Bright Productions LLC.

Dream Plan Series

For more information or to contact the author send inquiries to:

arlettethomasfletcher@gmail.com

https://www.arlettethomasfletcher.com/

To Dream

By Arlette Thomas-Fletcher

A **dream** is but a whisper in the recesses of our **minds**.

They can be **snatched** over the course of time.

If we wait too long, they **fade** away with the tide.

As the water returns to the ocean so can our dreams **drift** away.

But we must not let this happen because our dreams are **tiny diamonds shining bright** like stars in the night sky drawing us to look up at the beauty of the wonders they bring.

So, do not **fail the dream** by having no plan.

For every dream needs a guide to find its way to the **magical place** in your heart.

So be true and **faithful** to yourself and achieve your goals and make sure your dream has a dream plan.

Dreams are not to be **forgotten** or passed off as just mere chances.

But dreams are met to be **challenges** to something greater than ourselves.

If we must dream, let us **dream high** and reach for the sky never letting gravity pull us to the ground.

So, dream we must, but **work hard** too, so that we can make all our dreams come true.

DEDICATION

This book is dedicated to my mother, Inez Rosebud Thomas, who taught me to dream and that there was nothing in the world I could not achieve. My mother dreamed of raising her children to be the best they could be in life. She worked eighty hours a week for twenty years to assure her children's dreams were possible.

My mother saw two of her children graduate from Johns Hopkins University. Her dreams were realized for her children to have the opportunity to have dreams and for them to have the ability to follow those dreams.

She inspired all her children to work hard to achieve their goals and be the best they could be. She believed that dreams were important and that you should not let anything hold you back from going to college or getting training to have the desired career.

She was a loving and giving human being who always inspired her children, grandchildren, and anyone she could motivate to achieve their best in life.

To Kenneth, my husband, who has always supported me in achieving my dreams and goals for more than twenty years; Charles and Joel, my sons, who grew up dreaming and are now living the life that they dreamed of because of their hard work and faith in God.

ACKNOWLEDGMENT

Everything I write comes from the inspiration that the Lord has given me. I am truly excited about the opportunity to write this book. I want to honor the Lord Jesus Christ, my Savior, for giving me something I can share with adults so they can reestablish, strategize, and plan their dreams.

I am humbled to see my dreams come true by completing this book as an author. This would not be possible without the guidance of my Lord and Savior, Jesus Christ, who is the author and finisher of my faith. So, I would like to honor and thank God, from whom all blessings flow.

TABLE OF CONTENTS

FOREWORD

My purpose for writing the Restarting Your Dreams Self-Help book for adults is to help adults realize there is a difference between working a job to pay the bills and fulfilling their dreams.

This book is aimed at helping adults identify their dreams and make plans to achieve them, despite their age and experience.

This book outlines how adults can follow their dreams. Adults can go back to college and start a new career or leave a job after ten years or even twenty years to apply for other positions.

Working at a job you hate can adversely affect your health and mental state. Statistics show that 85% of people work in jobs that they hate. So, many people have been in careers for many years but are dissatisfied with their jobs.

Adults should know that they can start pursuing their aspirations at any age. As adults, we make decisions that we believe are best for ourselves and our families.

Sometimes, we choose a career that we think will work for us. Then it doesn't work out the way we thought it would. But because we have families to care for, we stay in the same career for thirty years or more. Often, we feel like when that time is over, we can't do anything else but retire.

I worked my job for more than twenty years and pursued my dreams simultaneously while I was a minister, wife, and mother. I am now doing the things I dream of doing with my writing, film, and singing. This took hard work and commitment to fulfill my dreams.

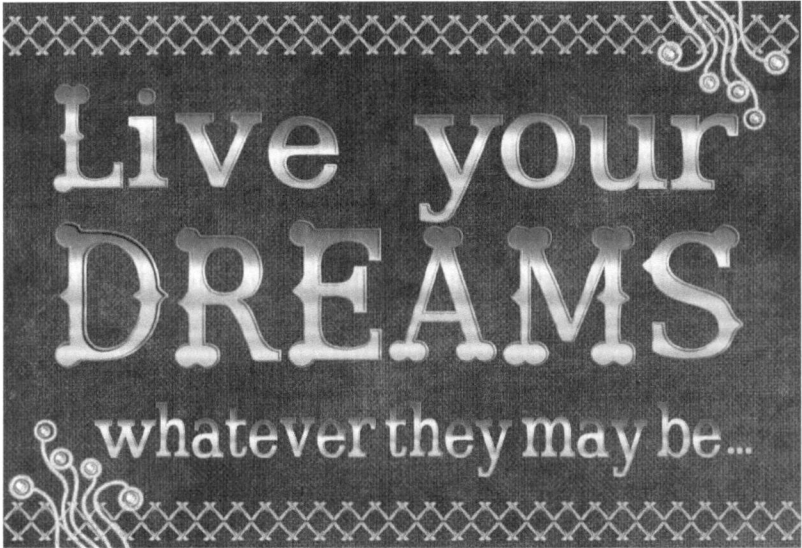

Live your DREAMS whatever they may be...

WHAT IS A DREAM?

A dream is a picture of what we want to achieve with our lives, which we create in our minds over time, from childhood to adulthood. A dream is a vision of who and what we want to be in the future. It starts from the mind and the heart. You cannot achieve what your mind and heart desire unless you allow yourself to be open to your dreams.

Dreams are woven together from childhood to adulthood. Somewhere along the journey from childhood to adulthood, we lose sight of our ambition. We often take the safe route where we are guaranteed a secure position doing something we are competent at achieving. But a dream is more than what you are good at doing.

It's more than what you're good at that makes a dream come true. Many people think that dreams are connected to what you are good at, and that is what you should do with your life. But just because you are good at raking the yard doesn't mean you should be a landscaper. Just because you are good at fixing cars doesn't mean you should be a mechanic.

As adults, we often find ourselves working for many years in positions that we are good at doing. Often, at the end of the day, we feel unfulfilled because our job is not what we enjoy doing. But it is easy to continue being employed in this position since we are good at it. Then, we begin to burn out over time because we feel empty at the end of the day. We want to do something else but are too afraid to try something new since we are afraid of failure.

Dreams begin when we are small children and stay with us until adulthood. As children, we are taught to use our imaginations, and there is no limit to the dreams we create in our daydreams. People often find their dreams in childhood fantasies that they indulged in while they were growing up. When they become adults, they may drop their fantasies since they have to face the reality of life. Dreams get pushed back into them as their life priorities press them to deal with their responsibilities.

Many adults were not allowed to express their dreams as children. They had a lot of things they loved to do, but they were not allowed to express themselves. Some people's dreams were quenched by their parents, teachers, or guardians. They may have considered those dreams unrealistic. They may have said they dreamed of being a supermodel one day as a child! But this may never happen because their parents told them it was an unrealistic dream. Some dreams may be unrealistic, but everyone deserves a chance to dream. Parents must encourage dreams, but if they do not, they can leave us with an empty feeling inside when we grow up to be adults.

Many people grow up not living the dreams they have woven into their minds due to many factors. This is the reason many people are frustrated with their lives.

If you took a survey of most people in the work world today, you would find that most people don't like what they are doing.

If you love running, then run and enjoy the peace and satisfaction that running brings to your soul. A person who loves running should not be confined to sitting in a chair every day looking at a computer screen. If you love the outdoors, then working in an office is not for you. You want to be able to travel and move around.

Doing something you don't like can lead to a lot of disappointment and frustration. It can also lead to stress and health problems. Sometimes, we get depressed as adults because we have not fulfilled our dreams or are afraid to take a chance to change our life path to do something different as older adults.

This is why dream planning is essential. Dream planning is about doing what stimulates your inner being, your soul! A great person once said, **"If you do what you love to do then you will never work a day in your life."**

When should a person start a dream plan?

A dream plan should be started when you are young, but it is not too late to start one now. Some of us started dreaming of what we wanted to do when we were five or so and stuck with that all our whole lives. However, most people start out saying, "I want to be a doctor, lawyer, model, or something else," and then, as they get older, their plans change.

It is not too late to restart your dreams now if you have not been living your dreams. You can still catch up with those dreams if you begin to plan for them now.

Ponder this:

A dream is the energy of the soul. It stimulates the mind for creative impact and achievements.

THE DREAM LAND

As stated earlier, dreams are woven together from childhood, but they are still with us through adulthood. A dream is not something that just jumped into you along the line. Dreams may have become passive in you due to many reasons, but it has always lived with you.

Many people grow up with ideas, pictures, and excitement about what they want to achieve with their lives.

There are events, places, people, and books that inspire and mold our dreams. Some traits and passions were ignited in us while growing up that inspired what we wanted to do with our lives. All these things are the dreamland from which dreams originate.

If you reflect and review your life over the years, you will discover there were pointers and indicators to what you should pursue with your life.

For example:

I find playing video games entertaining.

Maybe you should have been a video game designer.

You could also be a person that creates artificial intelligence that is used in military battles.

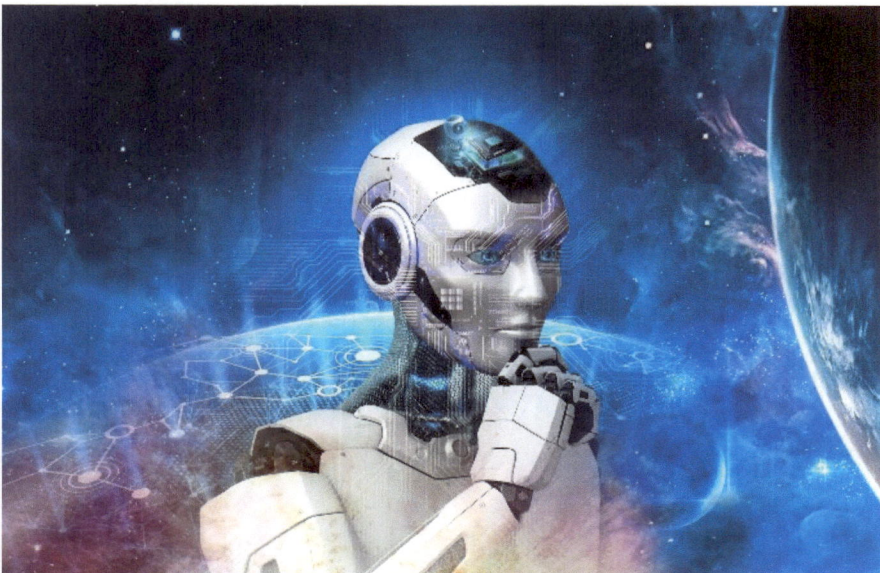

I like making sure things are secured.

Maybe you could have done cyber security.

Maybe you would be good at Homeland Security.

I am always thinking of how the food i eat at restaurants is made.

Maybe you should have been a chef or a cook.

I like helping people when they are in trouble.

Maybe you would be good at being a social worker.

How can I help you?

A fireman

A nurse

I like being outdoors around animals. I love to see the earth and its beauty.

Maybe you would be good at being a forest ranger.

An environmentalist

I love to look at the stars.

Maybe you would be a good astronomer.

These are examples of careers you could have pursued if you enjoyed these activities. Those pointers and indicators should guide the career choices of individuals.

People who are guided or allowed to explore these indicators end up achieving them in their lives.

The dream indicator has been seen in so many famous people, like Martin Luther King, Nelson Mandela, Lebron James, Roger Federer, Serena Williams, and many others. How do we know this? We know this because Martin Luther King's dream changed the world for civil rights. Nelson Mandela changed South Africa's way after Apartheid. Serena Williams became the first African American woman to win a Grand Slam singles title in the open era. She is also the second woman in history to hold all four grand slam titles at the same time. These are just a few of her achievements, which show that childhood dreams can come true.

My Personal Reflection

I started writing at the age of five. It started with me writing little plays. My sister and I would act out all the characters. I didn't take it seriously at first, but my sister made sure that I kept all the things I wrote. When I was older, I decided to write a poetry book, and some of the poems I wrote when I was younger were used in the book.

The book is called Poetry for the Soul. As I got older, I worked a full-time job, but I never gave up on my writing. I was amazed at how often I reflected on my childhood and the wonderful stories my sister, and I played out. I think the fun we had doing my little stories motivated me to continue writing. I will never forget the fun and laughs I had playing all those characters and the special time I had with my sister.

These are just some examples of dreams changing a person and the life of a society.

Ponder This:

Things you do effortlessly and passionately indicate what you should have aimed for as a career or profession.

REINVENT YOUR DREAM

Indeed, many adults are not living the dreams they formulated earlier. A lot of factors may be responsible for this.

Some people's dreams were quenched by the ignorance and insensitivity of the people around them. Parents, teachers, and guardians may have considered the dreams childish and unrealistic. This may have led to the abandonment of the dreams.

Some people get distracted by other people's dreams, which may seem better or more attractive than their own.

Some adults may have been pressured to take up their parents' careers or family businesses at the expense of their own dreams.

Some individuals got discouraged and had difficulties or hindrances on the path to accomplishing what they had set out to do.

Circumstances beyond their control hindered some.

As adults, we have different stories about why we could not pursue the dreams we once knew. Some of us got married right out of high school and had a family. This didn't leave us time to pursue our goals and dreams in life. Some may have just pursued a safe career in which they knew they would be successful.

In society, we are often taught to take the safest route in pursuing our careers. However, a truly happy and fulfilled life is spent pursuing what you are passionate about and not just what you think is safe to do.

As adults, we work all day and are tired from a long day at our jobs. We come home to families and responsibilities; somehow, one day blends into another, and then time escapes us. Then we find ourselves feeling like we are running out of time. It seems hard to commit time to your dreams when you work a full-time job every day.

Fear of trying to make a change in your career is also another barrier that can come up when making decisions to follow your dream. But, understanding that you are important and that you should invest in yourself by working on outlining all the reasons for pursuing your dreams is important.

Sometimes, isolation and lack of support can be barriers to pursuing your dreams as well.

To help combat this barrier, you can connect to someone working in the same career by attending networking events and joining associations that match the career you are interested in pursuing.

Below is a list of associations that cover just about any career you are interested in:

Accounting Associations

Architecture Associations

Arts Associations

Business and Economic Associations

Communications and Media Associations

Construction Associations

Counseling Associations

Criminal Justice Associations

Customer Service Associations

Dental Associations

Education Associations

Engineering Associations

Environmental Associations

Finance Associations

Health Associations

Human Resources Associations

Information Technology Associations

Sales Associations

Writing Associations

You can get further information about these associations by searching on the internet for the career you are interested in. Becoming a member of an association gives you access to the resources you need to be a success in your chosen occupation. It will also connect you to people that can further assist you in developing the skills necessary to achieve your employment.

You can still wake up those dreams, desires, and passions. You can reinvent your dreams by making plans to achieve them.

The first step to reinventing or restarting your dreams is to identify what your dreams were. Make a list of activities that you enjoy and would like to do every day of your life. Thinking about and writing about your dreams can stimulate your mind and activate your passion.

Then, make a list of the obstacles that have prevented you from pursuing your dreams. Identify how you can overcome the barriers that you have listed.

Also, state why you should begin to pursue your dreams now.

Make a list of what you will need to achieve your dreams now.

My Dreams:

_____

_____

_____

_____

_____

_____

_____

_____

_____

_____

_____

_____

_____

_____

_____

_____

Barriers to My Dreams

_____

_____

_____

_____

_____

_____

_____

_____

_____

_____

_____

_____

_____

_____

_____

_____

How to Overcome Barriers to Achieving My Dreams?

_____

_____

_____

_____

_____

_____

_____

_____

_____

_____

_____

_____

_____

_____

Reasons I Must Begin to Pursue My Dreams

_____

_____

_____

_____

_____

_____

_____

_____

_____

_____

_____

_____

_____

_____

_____

What Do I Need to Achieve My Dream?

_____

_____

_____

_____

_____

_____

_____

_____

_____

_____

_____

_____

_____

_____

_____

_____

_____

Ponder On This

A dream doesn't grow old. It can be achieved at any time unless a person believes their mind is too old to grasp it.

DREAM ENHANCERS & MOTIVATORS

All dreams are influenced by certain things, places, events, books, and films. These things are termed "dream enhancers" and "motivators." Visiting or thinking about them can stimulate your mind and bring back excitement and passion.

Some examples of dream enhancers and motivators are:

Diaries: If you are the type of person that used to jot down your plans, ideas, and fantasies, your diaries are good motivators. Take time to read the entries you have put down. There may have been some ideas you have forgotten over the years. So, going through your diary entries may help you to regenerate these plans again.

Reading them again will restore the excitement you have about them and stimulate your mind to think about pursuing them again. So, to restart your dreams, go through your diaries or journal if you have them. Something hidden in your diaries will revive the dream that has become dormant in you.

Vacations: Certain places remind us of some beautiful things. If you desire to restart your dreams, then take a vacation and visit those places where your dreams were first ignited. Some places are very majestic and enthralling, which motivates us because of the experience. Due to its fascinating scenery, the visit can rejuvenate us and move us to a different perspective on life.

Events/organizations: Organizations like sororities and fraternities help young men and women become leaders that cultivate social identity. Events held for students and alums at college associations, high schools, and college reunions are great ways to spark dreams. Connecting to old friends and colleagues is a good way to stimulate yourself to look at your dreams again. Going to high school or college homecoming games is also a good way of reconnecting with friends and thinking about dreams that you have wanted to pursue.

Books: Create time to read inspiring books, which can motivate you to achieve a positive mindset that focuses on your aspirations. If you dreamed of becoming an actor as a child and still desire it, find books about acting and filmmaking. Read books by authors who are doing what you dreamed of doing. Reading what others have achieved or are achieving in your desired areas can restore your passion for pursuing your abandoned dreams.

Documentaries: The media and the internet are full of documentaries of people doing great exploits in different areas. Take the time to look up these documentaries. They have documentaries on fashion, medicine, cooking, writing, gaming, and so much more. Spend some time researching and watching documentaries that speak to your deepest desires. It will motivate you to think about how to achieve what you have dreamed of doing.

Memoirs and Autobiographies: Memoirs are records of a part of the personal history of an author's knowledge and experience in life. People compile their inspirations, challenges, and successes to inspire others. Reading such accounts will inspire you to think about your dreams and ignite your motivation toward achieving them.

Autobiographies are usually about famous people like Chadwick Boseman, Paul Newman, John F. Kennedy, Barack Obama, and others. You can read how they achieved their position and what helped them succeed, as well as how they attained it. These books focus on the history of the famous person's life and are good resources for you to utilize as a guide for your life.

What inspired my dreams before?

_____

_____

_____

_____

_____

_____

_____

_____

_____

_____

_____

_____

_____

_____

_____

_____

Ponder This:

Your dreams have not died; they may just be dormant. Find the motivators to make them active again.

BALANCING DREAMS WITH REALITY

Many adults are not living their dreams. Many people have taken up jobs and careers that are not in line with their dreams. It is not so easy to go back to their dreams because they have the responsibility of a family depending on them.

It is difficult for people with many responsibilities to realistically make a move to leave their jobs or careers and start pursuing their dreams. But, over time, they can go to college or take training that will get them to their dream goals.

The best scenario for a working adult is to look at their options while employed. They should take the time to plan their lives, including the responsibilities that surround them. It may take a little more time to achieve their dreams, but with a plan, it is possible.

So, you must know how to balance the reality of your life and circumstances with your passion for pursuing your dreams.

Scenario:

You have chosen a career that is not in line with your dreams. For instance, you are a banker, and your dream is to be a choreographer. You already have a family and aging parents to take care of. How can you achieve this dream?

Start to do your research online about choreography and dancing. Go on YouTube and plan out your routines in your spare time. Work every moment that you have on getting your choreography training completed. You have to realize everyone has responsibilities, which does not mean your dreams can't come true. You just have to work harder. You will have to seize every free moment away from your responsibilities and work on your dream. It will take time, but you will achieve it if you don't give up on it.

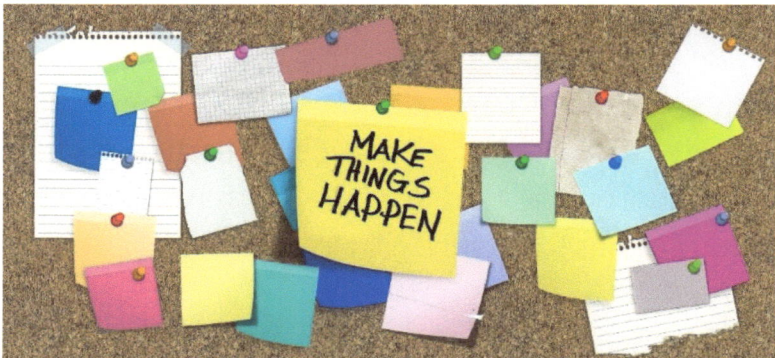

Decision:

Instead of watching television, sit down and research options for accomplishing your goals. You can enroll in an online or weekend dance school and participate in dancing challenges that will not hamper your performance at work.

This will give you exposure to your dancing talents. Make flyers that you can hand out at the dance challenge to get students so that you can teach dance routines.

This will also help you hone your choreography skills and get your name out there as a choreographer. You can also volunteer to give lessons at the Young Women's Christian Association (YWCA) or Young Men's Christian Association (YMCA) to work with kids, teaching them dance routines. This will also help you strengthen your dance and choreography abilities.

It is possible and achievable; it may just require extra work, determination, sacrifice, and resilience. Remember to also network with people in the career circle you are interested in, as they will be able to connect you to the resources that will help you move forward in your vocational dream.

Invite your family to your dance recital and your students' dance performances. This will allow your family to celebrate your achievements with you, making you feel secure in your dream and include them in your dream journey.

This will help them to understand why you are spending some family time away from them to work on your dream. You must be willing to make a short-term sacrifice to fulfill your long-term goals.

DREAM PLAN

What's your Life Scenario?

Life Scenario:

_____

_____

_____

_____

_____

_____

_____

_____

_____

_____

_____

_____

_____

_____

Options:

_____

_____

_____

_____

_____

_____

_____

_____

_____

_____

_____

_____

_____

_____

_____

Decision

_____

_____

_____

_____

_____

_____

_____

_____

_____

_____

_____

_____

_____

_____

_____

_____

Ponder On This

It doesn't matter how complicated things have become; you can rediscover and restart your dreams with a dream plan.

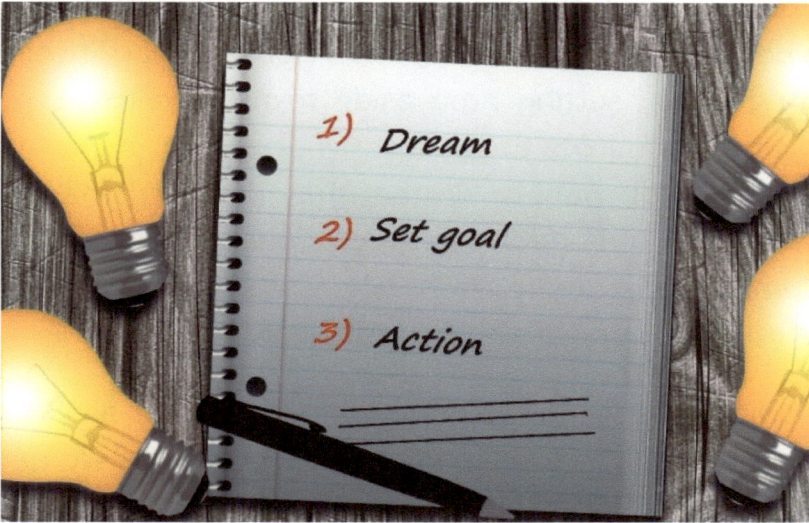

WHAT IS A DREAM PLAN?

A plan is a detailed proposal for achieving a goal. It involves stating the steps and methods required to achieve a goal. It also includes setting time aside and allocating resources to achieve a dream.

A dream plan is, therefore, all the goals and means you intend to achieve your dreams. A dream plan involves setting goals, setting time aside to achieve them, and allocating resources to actualize your dream. A dream is something you want to do that may be larger than life. For a dream to come true, specific goals must be set to accomplish the dream. Also, when reaching for dreams, one must be honest with himself/herself.

Organizing our targeted goals is important for achieving the aspirations that we have from the dreams we have outlined. Developed plans must be made to achieve the objectives to get us to our dreams. We have to look at dream planning as a strategy that requires active planning and structure to achieve our final purpose.

What does this mean?

All dreams don't always work out for everyone. Goals are important for achieving the aspirations that we have in our dreams.

Plans have to be made to achieve the goals to get us to our dreams. If we try to achieve our dreams and things are not moving in the direction of our dreams, we have to re-evaluate and determine if this is a possible and viable objective. We should always try for our dreams because it is important to know we tried, even if it does not materialize into what we want.

It is harder to accept that something didn't work out when you have never tried to see if it would work. Being honest with yourself is very important when making plans to achieve the goals that make your dreams come true.

DREAM PLAN

Jot down some of your goals

Short Term Goals

_____

_____

_____

_____

_____

_____

_____

_____

_____

_____

_____

_____

_____

_____

Long Term Goals

_____

_____

_____

_____

_____

_____

_____

_____

_____

_____

_____

_____

_____

_____

_____

_____

Ponder On This

If you fail to plan, you are planning to fail. Planning should precede all achievement. You cannot achieve your dreams by accident; you have to plan for them.

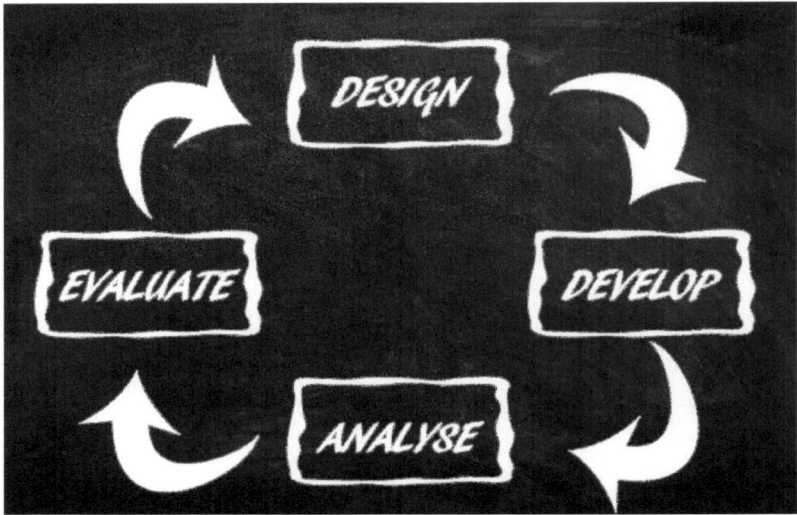

ANALYZE YOUR DREAM

As stated, several times in this book, planning your dreams is a necessary step toward achieving them. Another aspect of planning is analyzing your dreams, resources, and challenges. This involves doing **a SWOT** analysis. **SWOT** means strengths, weaknesses, opportunities, and threats. SWOT analysis is usually used for companies. It is designed to understand data that focuses on the strengths and weaknesses of an organization, which companies should use as a guide for improving the health of their business. An individual can also use this process to plan their dreams.

You need to analyze what your strengths are. Your strengths are in the things you love to do. They also include skills and knowledge you have that will help your dreams be achieved.

Weaknesses are flaws or areas that need work or improvement. It could also mean the skills you have not yet learned but need to develop through training and education. Remember, weakness doesn't mean you are not qualified for your dreams. It means you have areas to improve or need external help.

Opportunities are the favorable options that you have. They may include available resources and human support that are available to you.

Threats are challenges that can hinder you from achieving what you have set out to do. You should not be scared of the threats. You just need to identify them and plan how to overcome them effectively.

This analysis will help you to put everything into perspective and determine how to allocate your available resources to achieve your goals.

Number your lists in order of priority, 1-10, ten being the highest number.

LIST YOUR STRENGTHS

LIST YOUR WEAKNESS

Strengths

- I love learning new things.

- I can turn almost any negative situation into a positive one.

- I can make the impossible happen under pressure.

- I can get along with all different types of people.

Weaknesses

- I care too much about what others think about me.

- I hate cleaning.

- I procastinate.

- I have a weakness for trashy TV.

- I'm honest to a fault.

- Did I mention I hate cleaning?

_____

_____

_____

_____

_____

_____

_____

_____

_____

_____

List Your Opportunities

List Your Threats

Ponder On This

If you don't analyze your dream, you may never realize the usefulness of what you have and the things you need to work to improve.

DEVELOPING YOUR DREAM PLANS

LIST THINGS YOU LOVE TO DO

Make a list of things that you value. Take time to think about it and mow it over. Relax and just take your time and make the list as long as you like.

Nothing is silly; you are just trying to look at things you like to do. Don't worry about any order now; you are just brainstorming to determine how you feel about things. Sometimes, if you get stuck, don't worry about it; just take a drive, or go for a walk. This will stimulate you to think about your future plans.do

USE YOUR IMAGINATION

Start to look at the things you have put on your list that you adore. Begin thinking of yourself doing those things for the rest of your life. Start to daydream about how it would feel to do what you are fond of doing. Those that stand out the most are going to be the most important. Begin to research the types of jobs associated with what you are attracted to doing and would delight in doing every day of your life.

LOOK AT YOUR STRENGTHS

Begin to list all the things you think you are good at doing. Don't hold back because this is just to get your juices going. Remember, this list could be very long. Don't worry if it's short either. You can list anything on it, from being good at cooking to running a race. This is not a stressful exercise, so don't try and think too much. Just let all your ideas flow. You can ask your friends, parents, spouse, etc., about things you are good at if you need someone to verify these things with you. Remember, you are an awesome individual and want to feel good about what you do every day, which you can.

Admit you have Weaknesses

You may not be an artistic person who can draw, paint, dance, or even sing. Talent is not just in the ability to sing or dance. Talent can also be in the ability to build and construct something special. Talent can also be in doing a great report or coming up with an awesome process!

It doesn't matter if you are great at sports or any kind of athletics; what matters is that you have your own genuine skill that comes from the uniqueness of your make-up.

DREAM PLAN

Now that you have looked at the things you appreciate doing and everything you aspire to accomplish, it is time to move to your next step. Make a list of your strengths and weaknesses. Now, it is time to put your dream plan together.

Let's start with the things you are good at achieving. Maybe you are good at cooking, but you don't really like cooking. But your strengths are in creating recipes and writing. Possibly you like teaching others how to make new dishes, but you don't want to be the one to make them. So maybe you are a cookbook author. There are so many things you could do with this career. You could start a YouTube channel where you have chefs come on and create recipes from your book. This would give you exposure to cookbook recipes. Another thing you can do is do a podcast and have chefs come on and speak about your cookbook recipes. In addition, you can host customers who enjoy the food you make from your cookbook. The overall objective is to develop a cookbook that you are proud of and is marketable to people and chefs to spotlight their restaurant menu.

Maybe you enjoy an exercise class and just can't wait to get there every week. You also like dancing, moving, riding bikes, and being active. What if your current job requires that you sit behind the desk, staring at the computer?

You don't have to panic. You can still work around your job to fulfill your dreams. You can be a fitness coach, or you could open a fitness center. To do things like this, you often must start in an entry-level position and work your way up. But the key here is to do what you love and not just a job.

It is so easy to just go to school and focus on a major, but dreams are important, and we need to give space to our dreams. Some of the greatest people in history achieved their dreams through hard work and perseverance.

"J.K. Rowling had just gotten a divorce, was on government aid, and could barely afford to feed her baby in 1994, just three years before the first Harry Potter book, Harry Potter and The Philosopher's Stone, was published. When she was shopping for it, she was so poor she couldn't afford a computer or even the cost of photocopying the 90,000-word novel. So, she manually typed out each version to send to publishers. It was rejected dozens of times until finally, Bloomsbury, a small London publisher, gave it a second chance after the CEO's eight-year-old daughter fell in love with it.

Source: https://motivationgrid.com/

"Laura Ingalls Wilder, while growing up, repeatedly moved from places to places. With a desire to help her family, she decided to become a teacher. Laura Ingalls Wilder quits teaching when she got married and helped her husband on the farm. Following the death of their one-month-old son, her husband became partially paralyzed. She was 43 years old when her daughter, Rose encouraged her to write a memoir about her childhood. Her first attempt at the writing her autobiography has been rejected several times. Determined to succeed, she spent the next several years improving it. The publishers agreed to publish her work in a form of fiction story for young children. She was 65 years old when "Little House in the Big Woods" was published. She wrote other "Little House" series including the last one that came out at age 76."

Source: *https://medium.com/*

"Harry Bernstein encountered an unbearable loneliness after the death of his wife. This event served as the catalyst to start writing his first published book. Prior to writing it, he worked for different production companies as a magazine editor and freelance writer until the age of 62. He started writing the book, The Invincible Wall: A Love Story That Broke Barriers, when he was 93. It recounts his childhood experiences including the struggle his family underwent during World War I. The book was published when he was 96."

Source: *https://medium.com/*

"Gladys Burrill is truly one incredible woman. She had been an aircraft pilot, mountain climber, hiker, and a horseback rider. But these things are not what she is known for. She had her first marathon when she was 86 years old. She became famous after completing the Honolulu Marathon at the age of 92. Wait, marathon? 92 years old? Yessss! Though she power walked and jogged all throughout, she managed to reach the finish line. Even though it took her nine hours and 53 minutes to finish, she is proud of reaching the goal she set. She is determined to do it, and so she did. In turn, she was recognized by the Guinness World Records and Hawaii House of Representatives for her wonderful story."

Source: *https//medium.com/*

"Alan Rickman became a famous actor, but it wasn't easy as ABC. He took a degree in Arts because he said that drama school wasn't necessarily the sensible thing to do at 18. That led him to become a graphic designer, Rickman and other friends opened a graphic design studio. However, the calling of acting is strong, so he decided to drop the business and pursue acting professionally. He supported himself by working as a dresser for other actors. He got his acting break when he was cast as one of the leads in the stage version of Les Liaisons Dangereuse. The play was a hit and made a leap on the big screen. Unfortunately, he was replaced by another actor. He caught the attention of a producer on Bruce Willis' Die Hard. His passion and perseverance for acting served him well through various roles given. He is 42 years old when he took the role of Professor Severus Snape of Harry Potter series."

Source: *https://medium.com/*

"Anna Robertson expressed an interest in art since she was young. But she did not pursue it right away for several reasons – marriage and upbringing of children. She occasionally painted for a hobby, but she didn't devote time to it until much later. At age 67, she suffered a great deal of depression at the death of her husband. In order to cope up with the loss, she looked for ways to keep herself busy. In her seventies, she devoted most of her time to painting. She was completely self-taught. Her subjects were mostly about living the rural and agricultural life. Her first big break came when an art collector saw some of her works hanging in a local store and bought them all. She was 78 then. Her paintings were shown at the Museum of Modern Arts in New York. She later captivated the interest of a wider audience and became known as "Granma Moses." She was referred to as an American primitive artist and received several awards. She didn't stop from there though. She started writing her memoir, My Life's History at the age of 92. She died at the ripe age of 101."

Source: https://medium.com/

Ponder On This

Dreams are ageless. Put your dream plan together and restart that long-abandoned or dormant dream now!

NURTURING YOUR DREAM

DREAM PLAN

1. Take the things you love to do and determine the highest on your list based on the numbers 1-10. These are things that you would want to do every day as a job.

2. Look at the things you are good at and see if anything coincides with what you delight in doing.

3. Don't worry if you are not good at what you love to do.

4. Remember, you can get training and education to learn how to do what you are fond of doing, age is not a barrier. (Make sure it's realistic but don't limit yourself too much.)

5. Start looking at the goals you need to set to achieve what you have a passion for doing.

6. Begin to research the kinds of education and training that will be required to achieve what you are aspiring to be.

7. Align yourself with a mentor in the field that you are thinking of pursuing.

8. Ask the mentor questions regarding how they achieved their goals.

9. Remember that failure is a lesson in learning and does not mean that you should quit.

10. Analyze where you are at each step of your journey to reach the goals of your dream.

11. Surround yourself with people who are dream achievers, especially in the things you want to achieve.

12. Don't let negative voices interfere with your goals.

13. Remember to be rational and not set unrealistic goals or even dreams that may disappoint you because they are impossible to reach.

14. Stay focused and keep working on the plan even if it seems hard to do. Remember, this is what you want to do with your life but be honest with yourself. If you have done all the research to assure you that it will work for you, then you will already know in your heart if it is realistic for you.

15. Remember, it all has to be done in stages, so start with your dreams and goals. Make sure you incorporate what you love to do. Then make sure you

map out how you want to do it. Finally, the implementation of your dream plan is a process of combining everything you have worked on and putting it into action in your life every day.

Ponder On It

For your dream to come together, you must utilize all the components you placed on your list to have a great dream plan.

LIVING YOUR DREAM

Step I: Goals And Dreams

_____

_____

_____

_____

_____

_____

_____

_____

_____

_____

_____

_____

_____

_____

_____

_____

_____

Step II: What I Love To Do

Step III: How I Plan To Do It

Step IV: Implementation: Putting It Into Action

Notes

_____

_____

_____

_____

_____

_____

_____

_____

_____

_____

_____

_____

_____

_____

_____

Notes

_____

_____

_____

_____

_____

_____

_____

_____

_____

_____

_____

_____

_____

_____

_____

_____

Notes

Notes

Notes

Notes

_____

_____

_____

_____

_____

_____

_____

_____

_____

_____

_____

_____

_____

_____

_____

_____

Notes

_____

_____

_____

_____

_____

_____

_____

_____

_____

_____

_____

_____

_____

_____

_____

_____

_____

Notes

Notes

_____

_____

_____

_____

_____

_____

_____

_____

_____

_____

_____

_____

_____

_____

_____

_____

Notes

Notes

Notes

_____

_____

_____

_____

_____

_____

_____

_____

_____

_____

_____

_____

_____

_____

_____

_____

_____

Notes

_____

_____

_____

_____

_____

_____

_____

_____

_____

_____

_____

_____

_____

_____

_____

_____

Notes

Notes

Notes

_____

_____

_____

_____

_____

_____

_____

_____

_____

_____

_____

_____

_____

_____

_____

_____

Notes

_____

_____

_____

_____

_____

_____

_____

_____

_____

_____

_____

_____

_____

_____

_____

_____

_____

_____

ABOUT THE AUTHOR

RE-STARTING
YOUR DREAMS
FOR ADULTS

Arlette Thomas-Fletcher is a dreamer! While working a full-time job she has pursued her dream of being a writer, filmmaker, playwright, and vocalist. She was the president of Women In Film and Video of Maryland for ten years. She worked very hard to achieve her dreams. Over the years she worked on numerous projects. She was able to produce a sell-out play called "Daddy Where Are You?" at the Dc Black Theater Festival!

She has been able to produce her first Christian western feature film called "The Lonesome Trail" which has won many awards. Her Song "You're Not Alone" was the selection of the International Christian Music Awards. Her other song "Jesus You Are The One I Depend On" has been nominated for Best Performance Artist at the International Christian Film and Music Festival. She is now achieving her dreams by becoming an award winning screenwriter, songwriter, and filmmaker.

Since she was a child she has dreamed of writing stories plays, films, books and songs that would touch the hearts of people. In her life she has been able to accomplish her dreams by writing books, stage-plays, screenplays, song lyrics and articles. She is a minister of the Gospel of the Lord Jesus Christ and is humbled to be a vessel of God. Her work is inspired by God and she is humbled to have this talent to share with others. She believes that everyday is a new opportunity to reach your goals. She is a wife and mother of two wonderful sons. She truly feels honored to have them in her life and feels that they have been a true inspiration to her work by the support and love they give her every day. She has devoted her life to God for many years. She genuinely enjoys honoring the Lord Jesus Christ through the ministry in all forms of media.

This ministry is shown by her many works to glorify God in her writings, sermons, songs, and other works. It is truly an honor for her to pour out from her spirit what God has ministered to her to the people of God and the world at large. Arlette holds a Master's degree in Business from one of the most prestigious institutions in the country Johns Hopkins University. She also has a Bachelor of Science degree in Management Science with a concentration in Economics from Coppin State University.

9 780971 551084

OTHER BOOKS BY THE AUTHOR

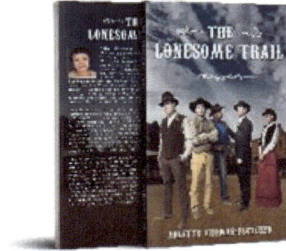

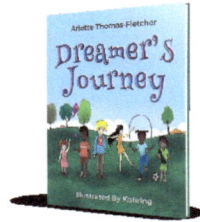

https://www.arlettethomasfletcher.com/